Pisa Travel Guide

Sightseeing, Hotel, Restaurant & Shopping Highlights

GW00809158

George Carpent

Table of Contents

Pisa

Pisa is a famous city in Italy that is best known for the world famous Leaning Tower but which offers much more. Pisa offers some of the most beautiful views of the Tuscan mountains and is just a short drive away from the scenic hill towns and villages of Tuscany.

Pisa was a bustling port in the 10th and 11th centuries. In 1944 during the Second World War, Pisa was attacked for 45 days. Thousands of its inhabitants were killed and half of the city's buildings were destroyed. Despite this the architecture, art and sculpture of the city are still its biggest attractions.

Pisa has retained so much of its historical look and feel that UNESCO has named it a World Heritage site.

Because the city center is quite small the best way to enjoy the sights is to walk the streets of the old city. Some of the most famous examples of architectural treasures in Pisa can be found in the Piazza deiMiracoli or Square of Miracles. This is a very large square with an immaculately tended lawn that has been there since the 11th century and which lies next to medieval walls that are still standing in the heart of the old city. The four marble buildings that rise out of that lawn combine the architecture of the Moors along with Celtic and Roman architecture and are some of Italy's most famous landmarks. The buildings include the cathedral known as the Duomo di Pisa, the world famous Leaning Tower of Pisa which was built as a bell tower for the cathedral, the Baptistery and the Monumental churchyard or Camposanto.

Throngs of travelers come to see these architectural marvels every year making Pisa one of the most important tourist sites in Italy. But that is not all that Pisa has to offer. The city also boasts several museums which are worth visiting for the architecture of the buildings themselves as well as the art and sculpture on display inside. Pisa's museums contain the works of many of the great Italian artists and are a must see for anyone with an appreciation of beauty and form.

The great physicist and astronomer Galileo Galilei was born in Pisa and his birthplace is still clearly marked and the city's international airport is named after him. Galileo attended the university in Pisa and studied for a medical degree before becoming a scientist. According to local folklore Galileo is said to have dropped objects from the tower of Pisa in an effort to see if heavier objects fell faster than smaller ones of the same material. There is no evidence to prove that this really happened but it is a great story to tell just the same.

Like pretty much anywhere else in Italy the food in Pisa is a gourmand's delight. Because it lies on the coast, Pisa is well known for its seafood dishes such as 'Bavettine Sui Pesce' which is flattened spaghetti seasoned with a delicious white sauce, mussels soup which is served on Tuscan bread and Frog soup. If seafood is not your favorite, however, the city also offers delectable land dishes and of course desserts, a favorite of which is the 'tortacoivischeri' which is a cake made with pine-seeds, raisins, chocolate and citrus candy. There is also a variety of local wines to accompany all the wonderful food.

Culture

Pisa is a university town with the University of Pisa students numbering 60,000 in a city that only 100,000 people call home. The university is one of Italy's oldest. It was established in 1343 and is considered one of country's best. Pisa is also home to the Scuola Normale Superiore an educational institute which has its origins in Paris and which has been around since 1810. Only the best students were admitted to this institute and it is still considered an elite school.

The city of Pisa has the vibe that all university towns have where you feel that a party can get started anywhere at any time and the students do often organize parties and other music events that are open to the public. There are of course nightclubs in Pisa as well as several pubs and pizza parlors such as the Millie Bar that boasts a vibrant Karaoke night every Tuesday because everyone knows that Italians love to sing. Many visitors enjoy just walking around the city center at night alongside the low walls around the river. Because it is a university city there are also always low priced accommodations available for the budget traveler.

Location & Orientation

Pisa is a city in the region of Tuscany, in Central Italy in the province of Pisa, close to Lucca and Florence. It is one of the chief towns in that region. It is located on the bank of the mouth of the River Arno on the Tyrrhenian Sea.

Climate & When to Visit

Pisa has warm, sunny summers as is common in the Mediterranean with the peak summer months of June to August being quiet hot and Pisa experiences temperatures of 30 degrees Centigrade regularly. In the wintertime it is cooler and quite wet and fog is a possibility. Although it doesn't really get very cold it can get windy so warm clothes are needed if you are going to visit between November and February.

If you are lucky enough to be in Pisa on the 16th of June you will witness the Luminara festival or Fiesta di san Ranieri. This festival is held to celebrate the city's patron saints day. In the evening of that day all the lights along the river go out or are lowered and 10,000 candles or torches are lit. There are also street events and fireworks displays. The city's monuments look even more beautiful by candlelight and this festival should not be missed.

One of the city's largest events is the Giocodel Ponte or Game of the Bridge which also takes place in the month of June and which has been around since the 16th century. The Game involves a series of challenges among twelve teams made up of people from the north and south banks of the city. They dress in medieval costumes.

Sightseeing Highlights

Piazza dei Miracoli (Square of Miracles)

56010 Pisa, Italy

The Piazza del Miracoli or Square of Miracles is a walled square located in central Pisa which dates back to the pre-Roman era. It is famous for the architecture of the building that can be found there as well as its cultural heritage and has been named by UNESCO as a World Heritage Site. It was given its name by the Italian poet Gabriele D'Annunzio who described the square that way in one of his books and is not to be confused with the Campo deiMiracoli in the fictional story of Pinnocchio.

The large square is also sometimes called the Piazza del Duomo after one of the buildings there. Made mostly of grass but with some paved areas, the Piazza is best known for the 4 marble buildings which stand in it and which are some of the most famous buildings in the world. All built between the 11th and 14th century, the four religious structures are the Duomo or Cathedral, the Campanile or bell tower, the Battistero or Baptistery and the Composanto or walled cemetery.

Apart from the four famous structures the square is also home to the OspedaleNuovo di Santo Spirito which was built as a hospital in the 13th century by Italian architect Giovanni di Simone. Its name translates to the new Hospital of the Holy Spirit but it is now home to the museum of Sinopias which you can visit to view the original drawings of the walled cemetery which is also located in the field. The hospital is made of red brick unlike the other buildings in the square which are white marble and it was restructured in 1562.

The Square of Miracles is considered to be one of the best places in the world for viewing and appreciating medieval art. Everyone who visits Pisa spends some time there and it is very easy to reach from either the airport or the train station.

Leaning Tower of Pisa

Piazza Arcivescovado, 6, Pisa

The Leaning Tower of Pisa is also called Le Torre Pisa or la Campanile (a bell tower that is free-standing).

It was built as the bell tower of the city's cathedral and the objective was to demonstrate the wealth of the city at the time. It is now considered one of the seven wonders of the Medieval World. When work began on the Tower in August of 1173, its design and the way it was being constructed was ahead of its time.

The intention was that the Tower would be vertical but after the 3rd floor was built it began to lean. The reason was not known at the time but it has since been discovered that the Tower was built on a clay mixture which was too soft to support the construction without sinking and the foundation was only 3 meters deep so the building began to lean in a southwesterly direction. Despite this, or perhaps because of it, the tower is considered the world over to be a great work of art and many people visit Pisa just to see it.

When the lean was first noticed in 1178, work on the Tower stopped. It began again in 1272 under the direction of Giovanni did Simone but stopped again in 1284 because of the battle of Meloria against the people of Genoa, Pisa's enemies at that time. The Pisans lost that battle.

The design of the Tower would be worth seeing even if it did not lean. The exterior is made of white marble and under the marble is limestone and lime mortar and it is that material that is most likely responsible for the fact that the building is still standing. The tower of Pisa rises 55 meters into the air and has 8 stories. The stories are made up of marble columns stacked on top of each other. There are over 200 Corinthian columns in all. The floors at the top of the tower were built out from the vertical in the direction opposite to where the tower leans in an effort to serve as a counter balance.

On the bottom story of the tower there are 15 marble arches. The tower weighs over 14 hundred tons, has 207 columns, 30 arches on each level above the ground floor and is said to be listing by about 10%. The inside walls of the cylindrical tower as well as the outer walls are made of limestone and it is hollow inside. There's a spiral staircase that is also made of marble and which is made up of 294 steps. The stairway goes up to the sixth level and in the actual bell chamber there are seven bells which are all properly tuned. The bells are housed in cells like windows. The bell chamber was completed in 1372 and work on the tower stopped after that until the 1800s.

When the bell tower was built 7 bells were put in. Each bell had a name. They were called L'Assunta, Il Crocifisso, San Ranieri, La Pasquereccia, Del Pozzetto, La Terza and Il Vespruccio. La Pasquereccia is the oldest bell. It was cast in 1262 by Lotteringo and carries an inscription that indicates when it was made and by whom. It also says that the bell was paid for by someone called Gerardo Hospilatarius.

The engravings on the bell include drawings of animals, angels and other religious depictions. Before it was put in the Tower the Pasquereccia was the bell used in the Tower of Justice to announce when criminals were being executed. It was most likely rung when Count Ugolino died. The bell weighs over 2000 lbs. and is also called La Giustiza. The largest bell is L'Assunta, named after Our Lady of the Assumption, which is made of gold and was cast in 1654 by Giovanni Pietro. It weighs nearly 8,000 lbs and carries an inscription that says "The angels raise the Virgin Mary to heaven and rejoicing and praising, they bless Our Lord."

The bells were rung using a bell cord from the ground but there was concerned that the swinging could affect the Tower so that was stopped. It was replaced by clappers within the bells that are activated by electromagnets.

Several people have worked on the tower but no one knows architect designed it. It was finished by Tommaso Pisano who built the belfry. In 1838 an architect named Alessandro Della Gherardesca decided to put in a pathway at the base of the Tower so that visitors could see the intricate work done on the base of the Tower. This made the building lean more.

In 1964 the Italian government led by Benito Mussolini, embarrassed by the continued leaning of the building asked for help and a team of professionals came together and decided to put in an 800 ton counter weight. They did this by drilling into the foundation and pouring in cement. Unfortunately the cement sank into the clay soil under the square and made things worse. The tower was closed to the public in 1990 in case the crowds make the leaning worse and it remained closed to visitors until 2001. The bells were removed and the building was anchored during that time. The engineers who worked on the Tower at that time believe that the building will remain at the angle it was then for several hundred years unless there is a major earthquake. It is currently open and a very popular site.

If you plan to visit the Tower it is a good idea to book your ticket online or in person a couple of weeks in advance so that you can avoid the long lines and that way you can also ensure that the tickets don't sell out before you get yours. People who book in advance also go straight to the top of the line. Advance tickets to climb the tower cost 17 Euros which is 2 Euros more than if you buy your ticket at the box office but you will definitely be able to climb the tower that day.

Twice every hour people are allowed in and if you buy an advanced ticket you will be allocated a certain time to enter. You have to ensure that you are there at the time. It takes about 10 minutes to climb the stairs and many people have reported feeling dizzy because of the tilt of the building. The Tower is opened from 10 in the morning to 5 in the afternoon from November to February except for Christmas day and January 7 when the tower opens from 9 am to 6pm. From March 21 to June 15 the hours are 8:30 am to 8:30 pm. For the rest of June and until August 31 the tower is open to the public from 8:30 am to 11 pm. All through September you can visit the Tower from 8:30 am to 8:30 pm while the schedule for October is 9:00 am to 7:00 pm.

Bell Tower of San Nicola Church

Via Santa Maria
56100, Pisa, Italy

Known by locals as Campanile di San Nicola, the bell tower at San Nicola church is sometimes overlooked because of the popularity of the city's other bell tower, the Leaning Tower of Pisa, but it is certainly worth seeing. Built in the Pisan-Romanesque style of architecture, the eight-sided tower is also found in central Pisa and is actually also leaning a bit. The base is already below the level of the road.

No one is quite sure when the tower was built but researchers believe it was built in 1170 and that Diotisalvi was the architect. Different types of stones, such as limestone, Elba granite and Apuan marble were brought in from different locations to give the tower its multicolored look. The marble was used to construct the columns.

Inside the tower is a spiral staircase which researchers recently discovered was designed based on the geometric studies done by Pisan mathematician Leonardo Fibonacci. The stairway has a wall on the external side only. The tower also has a roof that is shaped like a pyramid.

The bell-chamber of the tower has six sides and each side has a window. There is only one bell in the chamber. At present the public is not allowed inside the tower but the outside alone is worth the visit.

Duomo di Pisa (Cathedral of Pisa)

Piazza dei Miracoli
56010 Pisa, Italy

The Cathedral was the first building that was erected in the Square of Miracles. Construction began in 1064. The Catholic Cathedral is an example of Romanesque architecture although there are traces of other styles to be found on the building including the influence of the Arabs with whom Pisa had many battles. It was the spoils of some of these battles that were used to finance the construction of the cathedral. The Cathedral is one of the largest in the world and is nearly 600 years old. It is 30 stories high and has 464 steps which the public is allowed to climb. The outside walls are much more ornate than the inside.

The main architect of the structure was Buschelo and he is buried in the Cathedral. After him in the 12th century came the architect Rainaldo who built the white marble façade of the Cathedral. The stones on the exterior of the structure are engraved with ancient inscriptions. The Cathedral is sometimes referred to as the Primatial because the Archbishop of Pisa has been a primate since the year 1672.

In 1595 there was a fire in the cathedral that destroyed most of the medieval art that was displayed there. Luckily they were replaced by equally if not more beautiful works from the Renaissance era. Some of the original works survived the fire so there are also some medieval pieces such as the bronze door called the door of San Ranieri which was made in 1180 by Bonnano Pisano and which features scenes from the bible. The tomb of Emperor Henry VII which was done by Tino di Camaino in 1315 can be found in the cathedral as well as the bones of Pisa's patron saint Saint Ranieri. The Cathedral was consecrated in 1118 by Pope Gelasius II. Pope Gregory VIII was also buried in the cathedral but the tomb was destroyed by the fire of 1595.

There are many other works of art inside the Cathedral that are worth seeing such as an ornate pulpit by the Italian sculptor and painter Giovanni Pisano that depicts biblical scenes which is one of the Cathedral's biggest attractions and a crucifix by the sculptor Giambologna. The inside walls are made of black and white marble and there is a dome adorned with frescoes and a ceiling of gold which carries the coat of arms of the house of Medici. There is also a mosaic fresco on the wall above the main altar done by the great Florentine painter Cimabue with the help of his students. The Cathedral is also slightly tiled although unlike the Bell Tower it is hardly noticeable. All these pieces and more combine to make the cathedral or Duomo one of the premier edifices to visit in Tuscany.

Battistero (Baptistery)

Piazza dei Miracoli, 56126 Pisa, Italy

The official name of this structure which is also found in the square of Miracles is the St. John Baptistery and it is where baptisms were performed. The structure is the largest baptistery in Italy and is dedicated to St. John the Baptist. The Baptistery is taller than the leaning Tower of Pisa if the statue of John the Baptist at the top is included. The design is Roman but there is also evidence of Islamic influences and this is because construction on the baptistery started soon after the crusades. The Baptistery is made of marble.

Work began on this structure, which is nearly as big as the cathedral, in the year 1152 and was led by Diotisalvi. We know this because his name is carved on one of the interior pillars. Work stopped sometime after and a hundred years passed before work was again started on the baptistery because of a lack of funds. Construction was continued by Giovanni and Nicola Pisano and it was never finished until 1363. Because it took so long to complete, the baptistery has a mix of architectural styles with the lower portion being Romanesque and the upper section Gothic. The upper part of the building has the pointed arches associated with Gothic architecture while the lower portion has rounded gothic arches.

There are even two domes with roofs that are half lead, half tiles. The Baptistery is a circular building several floors high with a carved marble exterior and columns right around. Diotisalvi did not have that shape in mind when he began construction but when he died his successor Nicola Pisano changed the plans to a more Gothic style and it is he who added an external roof over the internal pyramid roof. The shape was supposed to resemble that of the Holy Sepulcher. Inside the Baptistery there are 8 tall columns and 4 pillars which form the central area. The roof is made up of a double dome which has a very unusual shape and which was added at the end of construction in the 14th century. The outer walls are very ornate while the interior has little decoration.

One of the main attractions of the Baptistery is a pulpit which the sculptor Nicola Pisano carved which can be found in the central area of the structure. The pulpit has six sides and on it there are scenes from the bible and other scenes such as one of a naked Hercules. It was created between 1255 and1260. On one corner of the sculptor there is a carving of Daniel that supports that side. There is also an eight sided baptismal font which was created by Guido Bigarellie da Como in 1246. It is next to the pulpit which is another big attraction along with a bronze sculpture by ItaloGriselli.

The artwork on the walls of the Baptistery depicts the life of john the Baptist and on the upper floors there is a depiction of Jesus Christ flanked by John the Baptist and the Virgin Mary with angels all around. A spiral staircase which takes you up the women's gallery and another staircase takes you right into the dome.

The acoustics of the building is one of the most fascinating aspects of the Battistero. It came about because of the double roof and every half hour or so a choir sings so that the sound can be appreciated. If you can sing feel free to try it out. Like most of the buildings in the Square of Miracles the baptistery leans slightly.

Camposanto (Walled Cemetery)

Piazza dei Miracoli, 56126 Pisa

Founded in 1277 the cemetery was intended as a place for the stone and marble tombs called sarcophagi in which local aristocrats were buried and that were scattered all over the nearby cathedral. It was completed in 1464.the legend states that the soil of the cemetery was brought to Pisa at the end of the Crusades by Ubaldo de Lanfranch. It is thought to be holy soil taken from Golgotha, the place where Jesus Christ was crucified.

The cemetery has 43 arches and 2 magnificent bronze doors by Ghiberti which are some of the main attractions. One doorway has a Gothic Tabernacle which depicts the Virgin Mary with child and 4 saints. The doorways that you would see if you visited the baptistery are replicas as the originals are in the Museo dell'Opera del Duomo in order to conserve them. The building also contains many statues and carvings of gothic design and sculptures

In the 14th century beautiful frescos were added to the inside of the walls. They were on the then controversial themes of Life and Death and were created by two artists who were very popular at the time, Francesco Traini and Bonamico Buffalmacco. These were later added to by other Italian artists who added stories of the saints and the Old Testament.

In the 16th century the tombs of members of the ruling Medici family and esteemed local university lecturers were also placed in the cemetery. It was later utilized as a museum.

During World War II, the Camposanto was badly damaged by a bomb dropped by the Allied forces in 1944. The bomb destroyed many priceless artifacts and efforts have been made to restore the building to its former glory and they have largely been successful.

Museo dell'Opera del Duomo

Piazza dell'Arcivescovado 8, 56126 Pisa (PI)

The Museo dell'Opera del Duomo in English means the Museum of the Cathedral Works and this museum houses many of the works of art that were formerly kept in the city's cathedral or Duomo. The museum is located where the Episcopal seminary used to be in the square of Miracles.

The Museum was created to display all the medieval art which was previously scattered all over the structures in the square. The museum has about 200 paintings that date from the 12th to the 16th century. Among its exhibits are the sculptures that were created by the famous Italian sculptors Nicola Pisano and Giovanni Pisano. One of the highlights of a visit to this museum would be the ivory carving by Giovanni Pisano of the Madonna and child which he made for the altar. There are also marble decorations that look distinctly Moorish in design.

After the war other works of art were placed in the museum and it is now home to a collection of religious garments, manuscripts and other items from the cathedral, including models of the Duomo, which make up what is called the Cathedral collection. There are also some relics from Italy, and Egypt as well as some Etruscan relics that had been on display in other buildings in the Square of Miracles since the beginning of the 19th century.

One of the highlights of the display is a wooden crucifix form the 12th century and a bronze griffin that was brought back from the Crusades. Be sure to see the sketches of the frescoes of the Camposanto that were made during the restoration in the 19th century. The restorer created etchings and his son colored them in. The Museum has the prints of these etchings that show what the paintings in the Camposanto before the bombing during the war looked like.

The art is divided into rooms with the pieces related to the architecture of the Cathedral such as models and plans, being displayed in the first room. The Romanesque art such as the 12th century crucifix and the bronze griffin are in room 3, while room six houses the statues by Giovanno Pisano and other precious items such as a cross that was used to lead soldiers to battle during the first Crusade.

Perhaps one of the best the best reasons to visit the Museum other than the ancient artifacts is the great view that you get of the leaning tower next door from the second floor courtyard. The price of admission for the Museum is 5 Euros. The Museum is open from 9 am to 7:30 pm Monday to Saturday and on Sundays from 9 am to 1:45 pm.

Museo Nazionale di San Matteo

Piazza San Matteo in Soarta,
Lungarno Mediceo, 56100 Pisa

Translated into English the name of this museum is the National Museum of St. Matthew. This museum is in a building on the waterfront north of the river Arno in central Pisa. The structure dates back to the 11th century. It was once a Benedictine convent and the original paintings are still visible on the walls. The museum collects religious works and has about 200 paintings. Some of the paintings and decorations on the walls are from the middle Ages and they have a distinctively Islamic feel.

Displayed in the museum are paintings and sculptures from the 12th to the 15 century from some of Italy's most famous artists including Madonna of Humility by Fra Angelico and St Paul by Masaccio. The museum also has as part of its collection Pisan sculptures from churches in the area that have been moved to the museum to protect them from pollution including several painted crosses. One noteworthy sculpture is a statue of the Madonna from the 14th century that was created by Andrea Pisano who is from the area. Copies of the sculptures have been put into the churches to replace the originals.

This museum is one of the most important in Europe for medieval art. It also has an important collection of art from Tuscany. The art is divided into sections with the sculptures and the older paintings being in the first room. There is also a section for manuscripts which are all lit including a bible with illustrations from the 11th century. It is definitely a place worth visiting and for 5.00 Euros you will certainly get your money's worth.

The museum opens from 8:30 am to 7:00 pm most days except for Saturday and Sunday when it closes earlier at 1:00 pm and Mondays when it is closed.

Palazzo dell' Orologio

Piazza dei Cavalieri
56126 Pisa (PI), Italy

The name means Clock Palace or Tower and you can find it in the Piazza del Cavalieri.

Inside the building is the Library of the ScuolaNormaleSupiore but in the middle ages the Palazzo had a very different purpose.

The Clock Tower was designed by Vasari and is made up of two buildings that were connected by a vault in the early 1600s. It used to be a place where old or sick Knights of the St. Stefano knighthood were sent. The two buildings were called the Torre deiGualandi and the Mansion del Capitano. When they were joined they were then named the Palazzo del Buon Uomo or Palace of the Good Man. In 1696 the clock which was formerly housed in the steeple of the church of St. Stefano was moved there and put in the arc that joins the two buildings. As a result the building was renamed to its current title. The small bell tower was put on the top of the building in 1696.

The building on the left is called the Palazzo della Giustizia, which was a tower house and in which could be found the offices of the city's magistrates. On the other side was the tower itself which was called dei Gualandi or Torre del Muda. The latter name refers to the eagle which is the symbol of the city. The tower has a tragic story and is sometimes called Torre della Fame or Hunger Tower because a nobleman, Count Ugolino della Gherardesca along with his family was killed by starvation while imprisoned there for treason. Legend has it that the count became so hungry that he ate the body of his dead grandchild. The poet Dante used this story in his epic the Divine Comedy.

The side of the Palace is decorated with frescoes by the like of Giovanni Stefano Maruscelli, and Lorenzo Paladini among others.

Campanile di San Nicola (St. Nicolas Belfry)

Via Santa Maria
56100, Pisa, Italy

This is the second most famous bell tower in Pisa and it is located in the historical center of the city. St Nicolas Belfry was intended for the church which is next door. Its design is in the Pisan-Romanesque style and it was built in 1170 by Diotisalvi. The Belfry has eight sides and is made of limestone and Elba granite with Apuan marble for the columns. The bell tower is a hexagon in shape with a window on each side. There is only one bell in the tower. There is a staircase in the bell tower that is winding and that has a wall on the outer side only. It is said that this staircase was the inspiration for the one Renaissance architect Bramante put in the Vatican.

The tower is not open to the public but there is plenty to see from the outside.

Museum of the Ancient Ships

Medici Arsenale,
Ponte della Cittadella,
Pisa, Italy

These ships were found in 1998 when workers from the National Railway Company were digging in preparation for building an electrical station near the Pisa- San Rossore train station.

They found the remains of a harbor and what later turned out to be 16 wooden ships which were later found to date back to between 200 BC and 500 AD. Some of them were very well preserved and investigations have led them to believe that the ships are Roman. They are the only ships of this kind to be found in such good condition. Some of the ships still had cargo on them. Some of the items found were tall Roman jars, called amphorae containing preserved fruit such as plums and cherries as well as olives. One boat had a leather sandal and a wicker basket. Archeologists who were brought to the site also found stone, iron and wooden anchors as well as ropes and fishing equipment. The finds tell a lot about life in ancient Etruscan and Roman times as well as life in ancient Pisa.

Although the official Museum of the Ancient Ships is still being constructed there is an exhibition that is open to the public every day of the week. On weekends you can visit without reservations if you go between 10am and 12 noon or between 2:30 and 3:30 pm. During the week reservations must be made. It contains examples of all the artifacts found including the personal items of the sailors. A tour of the museum will also teach you about the floods that led to the submersion of the harbor and the ships.

Ussero Café

Lungarno Pacinotti 27
Palazzo dell' Ussero
56126 Pisa

The Caffedell'Ussero is a coffee house in a red brick structure called the Palazzo Agostini which is located on the right side of the river Arno. The cafe is in a Gothic building that was constructed in the 15th century. Café dell'Ussero was opened in 1775 and gets its name from the Italian word ussaro which refers to a soldier in the cavalry. It is one of the oldest cafes in Europe. The word is originally Hungarian and came to Italy via France.

The cafe once had a reputation for being the meeting place of Pisa's scholars from the nearby university. It was also a favorite of the followers of the pro- politician Mazzini and some of the more liberal university lecturers. They gathered in the café to drink coffee, play billiards and discuss their political views. There is confirmation of these meetings in the town's police records from that time.

The café was turned into a cinema at the end of the 19th century. It was one of the first cinemas in the region. When the First World War ended Ussero was once again turned into a coffee house and the artists and literary types returned. Even today it is still a favorite haunt of the city's artists.

There are many stories of significant events that took place in this café and the walls carry testimony to many important and visitors. There are letters and other documents displayed that confirm the age and history of the establishment.

One of them the legends associated with the cafe is that in 1839 the Ussero café played host to meetings of the First Italian Congress of Scientists. The café has also seen other famous visitors such as the first director of the newspaper La Nazione, Alessandro D'Ancona and the Italian poet GuiseppiGiusti who talked of visiting the café in his memoirs. Other famous people who spent time at the Café include Charles Lindberg and the founder of the Futurist movement Gulieelmo Marconi. Many students from the local university spent time at the café and some of them have gone on to become Prime Ministers and Presidents and even receive the Noble Prize. There was even a collection of essays written about the coffee house called " L'Ussero: Un Caffe 'Universidario' nella Vita di Pisa". The café is open Monday to Friday 9am to 7pm.

Recommendations for the Budget Traveller

Places to Stay

Hotel Granduca Tuscany

Via San GiulianoTerme 13, 56017
Pisa, Tuscany, Italy
Telephone: (+39) 050815029
www.hotelgranduca.it

This is a fairly new hotel which has parking, Internet access and a restaurant where a buffet breakfast is included at no extra charge.

The Hotel Granduca is next to a sporting center and guests are allowed to use the heated swimming pool and tennis courts. The hotel also has its own Wellness Center.

Hotel Granducca has 170 soundproof rooms and every guest has a television, a radio and a telephone. Some rooms have terraces. The hotel is conveniently located near to the main train station and it is also close to the thermal spa of San Giuliano. The price of a double room is $57 US per night.

Hotel Capitol

Via Enrico Fermi 13, 56126
Pisa, Tuscany, Italy
Telephone: (+39) 5049557
http://www.hotelcapitol.pisa.it

This hotel is located in the center of the city close to the University of Pisa in a historic old building but with very modern furnishing. It is ideally located in walking distance of the main visitor sights and is also close to shops and restaurants so you can leave your car in the parking lot and walk to wherever you want to go. For the animal lovers pets are allowed at this hotel.

Hotel Capitol has an internal courtyard as well as a lounge area and bar. The price of a double room is $97 US per night.

Hotel la Torre

Via Cesare Battisti 17, 56126,
Pisa, Tuscany, Italy
Telephone: (+39) 05025220

Hotel la Torre is in the city center near to the sights that are on every visitor's list including the Piazza deiMiracoli and the Pisa Royal Palace. It offers free wireless internet, and satellite TV. and phones in every room as well as multi-lingual staff and a free buffet breakfast.

A single room with a private bathroom is $80 US per night and a double is $94.

Hotel Francesco

Via Santa Maria, 129, 56126, Pisa, Italy
Telephone: (+39) 050 555453
http://www.hotelfrancesco.com

Hotel Francesco can be found in the center of Pisa in a very old building that has been renovated to house the hotel. It is close to all the famous historical sites and to the airport. In fact it is on the same street that leads to the Leaning Tower.

The hotel offers free internet and phone calls, a large terrace, and a restaurant that specializes in Tuscan dishes. The price of a double room is $128 US

Eden Park Tuscany Resort

Via Enrico Fermi 11, 56126,
Pisa, Tuscany, Italy
Telephone #: (+39) 050870252
http://www.edenparkpisa.it

Nestled in the Tuscan countryside near to the river, this resort is still close to the City center and the main sights. It is consists of 30 apartments each with 2 rooms which are in cottages and is surrounded by forest. There are several medieval villages nearby and a great view of the hills. Each cottage has its own kitchen and private access.

The resort offers nature tours, horseback riding, and paragliding. It is the perfect location for couples or families that want to get away from it all. The price of a single is $82 US while a double is $ 41 per person and a triple $36. Breakfast costs $10

Places to Eat & Drink

Il Montino

Vicolo del Moule 1,
Pisa, Italy

Il Montino is a pizzeria that offers the option of dining in or having take out.

There are only a few tables so get there early if you intend to eat in. the cost of a slice of pizza is Euro 1.50 while the average price of a meal is between $21 and $29. The pizzeria is open from 10:30 am to 3:00 pm then 5:00 pm to 10:00 pm Monday to Saturday.

Ristorante Turrido

Via D. Cavalca 64, Santa Maria,
Pisa, Italy

This indoor/outdoor restaurant is 20 minutes from the
Leaning Tower and is known for its Tuscan dishes
especially its pesto. The locals eat there and there is
usually no better recommendation. This restaurant is also
known to offer a wide array of desserts. It's open
Monday to Saturday 6:30 pm to 10:30 pm

Peperosa Pisa

Via Renato Fucini N 10, 56126
Pisa, Italy
Telephone: (+39) 0503144170

The eatery offers Italian and Mediterranean fare and also
has a wine bar. It is recommended that you make
reservations. Prices for a meal range between $13 and $39
US and Peperisa is open Sunday through Saturday 11:00
am to 3:30 pm and 7:00 am to 12:00 midnight.

L'Ostellino

Piazza Felice Cavallotti 1
56126 Pisa

This diner is known for its sandwiches as it has a very wide assortment of fillings and fresh vegetables. Most of the sandwiches are available for between $4 and $8 and there are also meals available. L'Ostellino also has a bar so everything you need is in one place. The dress code for this diner is casual and no reservations are necessary. The restaurant does take out but not delivery and be sure to walk with cash or a debit card because credit cards are not accepted.

Coccio Bar & Gelateria

Via Santa Maria 86,
Pisa, Italy

This little restaurant specializes in local Italian cuisine and ice cream. It's near the leaning Tower and is known to offer a delicious breakfast. This eatery is known for its cappuccino as well as its salad. Coccio also serves sandwiches and other typical café food. Most of the fare at Coccio Bar can be had for under $10 US and the staff has a reputation for being very courteous and quick.

Places to Shop

Corso Italia

The Corso Italia is the High Street of Pisa with many shops and a lot to offer the shopper who does not want to spend a deal of money. It is usually a very busy and crowded street in the quarter of San Marino. On this street is a commercial center called the Corte di San Domenico. Further down the street near to the river a monthly antique market is held in a 17th century building called the Logge dei Banchi which used to be a jail.

The Corso Italia is also a good place to get a trendy haircut or buy a comic book for a specialty shop known as Fumettando. After working up an appetite from all the walking you can grab a slice of Pisan pizza or even buy a Nutella wafer.

Borgo Stretto

This street offers high-end shopping and boasts expensive shops and boutiques. Take a walk under the archways and watch the lovely window displays. When you need a break from shopping there are many cafes and ice cream parlors. Examples of shops to be found on this street are Valenti which has been in business since the 70s and which carries the latest in designer fashions for men and women and BB Maison. There are also stringed instrument shops that are a must for any visiting musician.

If you happen to be in Pisa at Christmas there is a market on Borgo Stretto where you can get some of the designer duds for less. There are also markets and shops on the side streets off of Borgo Stretto that offer better bargains.

Piazza dei Cavalieri & Ponti di Mezzo

There are open markets on these streets on the 2nd weekend of every month. These markets are a good place to find antiques at an affordable price. If you find something that appears to be too good a deal then it probably is so be very careful about what you purchase. It should be noted that the markets do not open in the months of July and August.

Piazza delle Vettovaglie

Scaliaureliosaffi
Livorno, 57123

This square is over one hundred years old and houses many shops as well as a fruit and food market. This is a good place to purchase wines and grocery items. It is also called the Central Market and is the largest indoor market in Europe. It is a covered market and is always very busy with people looking for fresh fruit and vegetables. Do not miss an opportunity to try the bread on sale especially the Tuscan 'saltless' bread or the star of the market the labronica or Pavilion fish which has been extremely popular for many years.

There are over 200 shops in the market as well as scores of wineries in the basement which can be accessed from two side doors and down the stairs. The market is also a wholesale market. There are also bars and cafes and it is open Monday to Friday from 7:00 am until 1:30 pm.

Via Buonarroti & Via San Martino

If you are looking for thrift shops and bargain shops then these two streets are the place to go. Via Buonarrotiis a busy market and both street markets open every Wednesday and Saturday. You can find clothes at these markets as well as fashion accessories and other items. Via Buonarroti offers many souvenirs and is one of the places where the locals shop.

CPSIA information can be obtained
at www.ICGtesting.com
Printed in the USA
LVOW10s1533090217
523756LV00034B/934/P

Introducing Cornwall

B Trevail

Tor Mark Press · Penryn

Jamaica Inn, Bolventor

This edition first published 1990 by Tor Mark Press,
Islington Wharf, Penryn, Cornwall TR10 8AT
© 1990 Tor Mark Press
ISBN 0-85025-319-5

Acknowledgements

The publishers are grateful to the following for kind permission to
reproduce illustrations: Cornwall Local Studies Library, Redruth
page 20; Men-an-Tol Studio page 29; Royal Institution of Cornwall
pages 1, 8, 34, 36, 40, 41, 43, 44; Paul White cover, pages 2, 4, 7,
10, 13, 16, 18, 24, 27, 32, 38.

Printed in Great Britain by Swannack Brown & Co Ltd, Hull

Mines beneath the sea

In the nineteenth century, Cornishmen responded to the lure of a deposit of ore like iron filings to the invisible pull of a magnet. Both tin and copper were mined in conditions which might have deterred a people less imbued with the spirit of mining; problems such as great depth, costly drainage, dangerous ground and financial risk were welcomed as challenges and in most cases were overcome.

Nothing better illustrates Cornish skill and tenacity in mining than the various mines which have been worked out to sea, beneath the coastline of the county. First and foremost was the celebrated Levant Mine, on the cliffs north of St Just, which exploited lodes running westward under the Atlantic. In its main period of activity, Levant was worked from 1820 to 1920 and at the end of this time the deepest levels extended a full two miles out under the sea, approximately 350 fathoms below high water mark. At this depth even steam engines and, for a brief period, locomotives worked, hauling ore back to the foot of the shafts sunk vertically from the cliffs. Since mining ended at Levant (in 1930) the sea has broken in at a weak point in one of the shallow levels beneath the sea-bed.

Botallack is an equally famous mine adjoining Levant, where the miners followed tin and copper lodes far out beneath the sea. But here a shaft was sunk at an angle to meet these submarine lodes in depth. Various photographs have been published of this diagonal shaft, which was visited by Royalty in the 1860s. Other mines along this stretch of coast have also pushed levels out many yards seawards, and there are tales, probably true, of miners at work during gales hearing the noise of stones rolling on the seabed above their heads. Wheal Margery, a mine between St Ives and Carbis Bay, and Trewavas Mine, situated on a headland near Porthleven, are other mines with submarine workings. Like Levant, Trewavas eventually suffered from an irruption by the sea which terminated mining there about 1860, fortunately without loss of life.

A submarine mine of a different kind was worked beneath the waters of Restronguet Creek, one of the tidal arms of the Fal estuary. Here alluvial tin was won from strata under the bed of the creek — a unique occurrence apart from similar workings under the tidal sands near Par.

Offshore from Penzance, on a tidal reef, was the Wherry Mine, worked on more than one occasion in the period from 1770 to 1840. A shaft was sunk into the ore-bearing rocks here, with a protecting wooden structure around it to keep out the sea, the whole being connected to the shore by a long bridge. A vessel which broke from its

Wheal Trewavas, an undersea mine closed by flooding about 1860

moorings in a gale in the 1790s smashed this down and the mine was inundated. Then in the 1830s the Wherry Mine was revived, this time having a steam engine on the shore for pumping via connecting rods out to the shaft which was, at high tide, surrounded by the sea.

In east Cornwall, more than one mine has been worked under the waters of the upper Tamar estuary for lead. From the Devonshire bank, near Weir Quay, Tamar Consols had levels which ran at great depth over half a mile beneath the river. The nearby South Tamar Mine also explored the same area until, in August 1856, one of the shallower levels collapsed and completely flooded the mine. Fortunately it was a Sunday and no-one was underground or there would have been a serious loss of life. As it was, the mine was irretrievably ruined and could never be worked again: an end that is always a fateful possibility in a mine beneath the sea.

The old wreckers

The existence of 'wreckers' in Cornwall in olden days is disputed by many, being held by some to be a gross calumny upon a county which, though it might countenance smuggling, would not descend to luring ships to destruction for the sake of cargo. Certainly no historical record remains of anyone apprehended for such a crime, but that does not mean it was never perpetrated. The tale of wreckers tying a lantern to the tail of a cow or donkey so that it swung to and fro like a vessel's masthead light as the animal wandered along the cliffs on a dark night is unlikely to be sheer fabrication and as a method of bringing vessels too close to a dangerous coast would take some improving upon.

But this sort of wrecker, if he existed at all, was rare. Much more common were the wreckers who descended like vultures upon a ship once she had been wrecked, plundering cargo, ship's fittings, and even — on more than one occasion — the remnants of the ship's timbers as well. These are the wreckers who assuredly did exist and whose depredations made Cornwall a by-word amongst seafarers in the eighteenth century. Every seaboard county in Britain had its wreckers of this type but the population of Cornwall seems to have been particularly lawless. This may have been due to the remoteness of the county in former times and the inability of the civil authorities to prevent plundering. At times of severe gales, when several vessels were flung ashore along one stretch of coast, such as Mount's Bay, the coastguard or magistrates were unable to attend more than one of these at a time.

Once news of a wreck, or of an impending one, spread like wildfire through a coastal district, people gathered by the hundred on the cliffs. Men would come hurrying from the mining districts inland, eager for their share of this occasional harvest of the sea. This was particularly the case in the parishes along the coast between Marazion and Porthleven, a part of the south coast where numerous wrecks took place, and along the north coast by Camborne and Illogan. The crowds followed a stricken vessel along the coast, speculating where she would eventually be driven ashore. And then, no matter what the state of wind, weather or tide, and no matter how dangerous the cliffs, the bolder spirits were upon the wreck, dodging the waves and fervently hoping she carried a cargo of real value. If, as was frequent on the north coast, she was from Ireland, they hoped for butter and sides of bacon — not oats — when her holds burst open; on the south coast, they hoped for a Frenchman, with cloth perhaps, or better, with kegs of spirit or tuns of wine. Then wrecking fever really seized hold and even those who had assembled merely as spectators joined in the fray. A few might join in efforts to save the lives of sailors aboard but it was not for such a purpose that the more determined elements of the assembling crowds carried axes, ladders and ropes. As well as the cargo, everything of the slightest value that was swept by the waves off the wrecked vessel was carried away; rigging, spars, bulwark and hull timbers, hatch coamings, cabin doors and the like were all carried off as prizes.The Customs had little hope of recovering much of this subsequently, indeed they tried hard only when the stricken vessel carried a valuable cargo of highly dutiable goods. Tales are numerous of the efforts they made to locate hidden caches of plundered wine and spirits but on such occasions they were also up against the Cornishmen's undoubted skill in smuggling and hiding smuggled goods — but that is another story.

Wrecking of a very harmless kind persists even to the present day, though more accurately it might be termed beach-combing and the recovery of flotsam rather than true wrecking. Probably the last vessel to provide Cornishmen with much forbidden fruit of the sea was the *Bessemer City,* a large American steamer which was wrecked west of St Ives in November 1936. Her hull broke open from the pounding of the waves and much of her cargo subsequently washed out of the holds and so onto the dining tables of very many homes in and around St Ives.

Did wreckers like this ever exist? Probably not, except in the vivid imaginations of writers and artists

Cornish china-clay

'Fish, Tin and Copper' used to be the toast of Cornwall in the nineteenth century when mining and the sea provided the day-to-day livelihood of almost everyone in the Duchy. At the present time all these former staples have passed into history and the most important industry left in the county — if one excepts that of catering for the holidaymaker — is the production of china-clay. It is curious that this industry has grown and prospered enormously during the self-same period that metal mining in the county has dwindled from world predominance to negligible proportions. The key to this situation lies in the fact that Cornwall has, and is likely to retain, a monopoly of the

7

China clay ready for shipment, 1906

finest china-clay deposits in the world, whereas she has lost for ever her near monopoly of copper and of tin.

China-clay is a constituent of decomposed granite and occurs throughout much of the moors north and west of St Austell. Originally it was worked here, from the mid-eighteenth century, for the making of pottery, but the industry expanded enormously after 1870, when china-clay began to be used as a filler in cheap printed textiles as well as in the manufacture of paper.

Everywhere in the clay district is white: the men, the houses, the dumps, the pits themselves, even the very rivers. Some of the pits are of enormous size, rivalled only by the great conical 'sky dumps' of waste quartz sand beside them. These latter represent the principal problem of the industry, for about nine tons of the waste have to be dumped for every ton of merchantable fine clay. Powerful hydraulic monitors, like fire-hoses, are used to break out and wash the clay from the sides of the pits, and this is then pumped to surface as a slurry. After various settling processes, the finest clay is left in suspension and then goes through a series of drying operations. Big, coal-fired 'drys' were once common throughout the district but much clay is now dried by rotary warm-air blowers having much greater throughput and efficiency. Finally, in former times, the dry clay was casked ready for carting to the port of shipment but today is either bagged or consigned thence by lorries in bulk. Pentewan, Charlestown, Par and Fowey were all used but only the latter two are active on any scale today.

The industry was once the province of several dozen firms, each with a pit or two, but after a series of mergers three or four larger companies had emerged by the end of the nineteenth century. Output continued to keep pace with the ever-growing needs of a variety of industries, with china-clay finding a number of new uses as technology advanced: in pharmaceuticals and in the making of plastics, inks, insecticides, paints, rubber, cosmetics and a host of other products. A wave of mergers following the First World War resulted in the emergence of English Clays Lovering Pochin and Co Ltd, a combine of most of the former principals in the industry. Today English China Clays Ltd has a near monopoly, running the industry efficiently as a single unit, concentrating on the exploitation of fewer but larger pits and with its own port, Par, for the efficient despatch of much of its output.

Cornwall has lost, probably for ever, her former greatness in the mining of tin and copper but in one other aspect of mineral extraction occupies a unique position with her unrivalled china-clay deposits. The strange lunar landscape of the china-clay country to the north of St Austell is a rare and well-nigh unique sight anywhere in the world today.

Roche Rock

On the southern edge of the great, peaty upland flat known as Goss Moor, south-west of Bodmin, lies the ancient village of Roche, which has taken its name from the remarkable crag of rock just beyond the houses, where the wild moorland begins. A landmark for many miles around, on account of the way in which it towers above the surrounding level countryside, this strange rock outcrop is of interest for several reasons.

Roche Rock is really an off-shoot of the great mass of Cornish granite to its south, which forms the St Austell Moors and the china-clay country. Just as china-clay rock is actually a type of granite, so also is this remarkable crag — a type in which large quantities of black, radiating, needle-like crystals of the mineral tourmaline occur. The Cornish call this 'schorl' rock, and a specimen is worth acquiring from this vicinity.

Roche rock and chapel

An equally remarkable feature of the rock is the fifteenth century chapel of St Michael, with its hermit's cell, perched on the summit. Built of granite, the sturdy little building seems to grow out of the very rock itself. There are steps leading up to the chapel, and the view from the top, across the lonely wastes of Goss Moor towards the ancient hill-fort of Castle-an-Dinas, and southwards towards the china-clay country, is rewarding.

Cornwall abounds in legends, and the Goss Moor is not without its share. The fearful spirit of Tregeagle, who haunts Cornwall from coast to coast, pursued eternally by fiends or by His Satanic Majesty and his headless hounds, came here to Roche Rock long ago in search of refuge. Escaping from the endless penance for his sins that he had been given to perform at Dozemare Pool on Bodmin Moor, he fled howling through the darkness over the moors and thrust his head through the tiny chapel window, into sanctuary. Hating equally the hermit's holy words within and the shrieks of the thwarted demons without, he howled louder than the winter tempests, keeping all the villagers of Roche awake and trembling; none of them dared venture near the holy place. Eventually Tregeagle was removed by holy men using magic spells and taken far away to the north coast, where he was set to the endless and hopeless task of making ropes of sand at the restless tide's edge.

The lost land of Lyonesse

About twenty eight miles off Land's End lie the Isles of Scilly, of which there are some two hundred. Only five of these are inhabited today, most of the remainder being too small and rocky or too difficult of access in winter seas ever to have been lived upon. It is an unusual experience even to the island Britisher to watch this vast fleet of rocks vanish one by one beneath a rising tide; at low water they are to be numbered in hundreds, whilst at high relatively few remain and there is perhaps for the more imaginative a brief feeling of panic as the inexorable rising of the water continues. The sea between these many closely grouped islets, a clear and marvellous blue in summer but in winter a seething mass of treachery, is thus so shallow that only the slightest elevation of the sea-bed would make of them one many-pinnacled granite island. In the same way, the waters between Scilly and Land's End are none too deep and the slightest uplift of the ocean floor here would also produce dry land — and so there would re-emerge once more the magical and long-lost land of Lyonesse.

For legend has it that such a land once existed: a land of great fertility, inhabited by a beautiful race of people who built many splendid cities (does not the dreaded Seven Stones reef mark the site of one of them?) and some 140 equally marvellous churches, whose bells from time to time may be heard beneath the sea, gently tolling with the rocking waves. One single night, some 900 years ago, the whole of Lyonesse was overcome by a vast inundation from the sea, which flooded over all but its highest peaks, catching the sleeping people unawares and engulfing the cities and churches in rapid succession. It is said that only two living creatures survived this disaster: a man named Trevelyan of Basil, near Launceston, was able to flee before the rising wall of water on his swift white horse and reached dry land safely at Perranuthnoe.

And so Lyonesse disappeared, engulfed by a wide stretch of glittering sea that separated the cliffs of the newly-created Land's End and the just-born Isles of Scilly barely visible on the far horizon. Mount's Bay fishermen at one time — and perhaps still — would tell you that on clear nights near the Seven Stones the roofs of houses were visible beneath the water, whilst there is other more down-to-earth local corroboration, both historical and geological, of the drowning of Lyonesse. A Saxon chronicler even states that 'the Lyonesse was destroyed on 11 November 1099' — but then who wants proof; we must all be permitted to dream.

Cornwall's holy men — the Saints

It is said of Cornwall that she has more saints than has heaven itself and no-one can travel far in the county without becoming aware not only of some reasonable justification for this claim but also that the names of these holy men and women to whom so many parishes, towns, villages, churches and holy wells are dedicated, are certainly not found in the Bible, and in fact are rarely even the familiar names of the Western Christian Church. By the hundred these peculiar names occur again and again in every book on Cornwall, on every map of the county, and on multitudes of guideposts from the Devon border to Land's End. Few things indeed are more singularly Cornish than her band of saints.

The reason why Cornwall is so different from the rest of the country in this respect is purely historical. The Christianity which came to much of Britain when the Romans invaded this country from Gaul was subsequently suppressed by the heathen English (Saxons), who also entered Britain from the east. But the heathens failed to stamp out Christianity in the remoter and more mountainous west — Wales, Cornwall and Ireland — and so it was that until the English themselves became converted to Christianity after AD 597 only this inhospitable western Celtic fringe remained Christian.

There were heathens enough in Cornwall however, this being less impregnable than either Wales or Ireland, and the Christian faith here was strengthened by the arrival of numerous missionaries from Ireland — the 'Land of Saints' — and to a lesser extent from Wales and Brittany, chiefly during the fifth and sixth centuries. They came to convert the people, and in the process founded many of Cornwall's numerous churches.

These Celtic missionaries, with their characteristic staffs and little holy bells, are surrounded by legend, and authentic historical facts are few and very precious. It appears that the Irish saints arrived in the fifth century and landed somewhere in the Hayle estuary; the names of several — St Breaca, St Ia, St Germochus, St Gwithianus, St Wynnerus — are preserved in the parishes of Breage, St Ives, Germoe, Gwithian and Gwinear in this same area. There was also St Buryan, the female saint of the Land's End; St Ruan, whose oratory lay in a wood full of wild beasts; St Uni, patron saint of Lelant and Redruth; and of course St Piran or Kieran, who arrived on a millstone and whose tiny oratory still stands under the sand-dunes north of Perranporth. This is one of

The church of St Ia, St Ives

the oldest Christian buildings in Britain. Then there was St Feock, whose church lies in an idyllic setting on the banks of the Fal, and who arrived safely in this spot from Ireland floating on a granite boulder.

Rather naturally, the Welsh missionaries arrived principally on the north coast; St Petroc and his three friends, for instance, who crossed the Severn sea safely in a little boat like a Welsh coracle, negotiated the dreaded Doom Bar and entered the Camel estuary. St Petroc himself was destined to have four churches dedicated to him, one of these at Padstow (anciently Petroc-stow) itself. Similarly St Carantoc, who lost his stone altar overboard during his passage of the Severn, retrieved it with the help of King Arthur and set it up at Crantock, south of Newquay. St Morwenna of Morwenstowe and St Keyne, famous for the holy well of that name, were female Welsh saints, whilst two of the Welsh holy men came finally to rest after their wanderings on the shores of the Fal, on the south coast. St Kea dreamed he must go to Rosynys — which was Roseland — and when his holy bell rang, there set up his church, but the old Kea church in fact lies opposite Roseland, on the western shore, and is now in ruins. Closer to the open sea, and on the eastern bank, are the church and holy well of St Mawes, tenth son of an Irish king, although he came from Wales. There were also a smaller number of Breton saints whose influence was strongest on this same southern shore — for instance St Cury and St Winwalloe.

In common with other Celtic races, the early heathen Cornish venerated wells and springs. The Christian missionaries from Ireland, Wales and Brittany made clever use of this fact to effect a transition in the minds of their potential converts to the Christian religion, making the water sources baptisteries, or otherwise consecrating them. Near these wells or springs they erected hermit cells or chapels, often of wood, in spots that were frequently very remote. These cells were later replaced by Celtic monasteries or by that phenomenon of Cornwall, the isolated church outside the parish boundary and far from a nucleus of settlement. Some one hundred holy wells, many called after a Cornish saint, are found in the county and a considerable number have delightful little buildings over them. It must be said that many still have strange healing and other powers which have scant or no connection with Christianity, such as Ludgvan well, where a dash of the water ensures that your offspring will refrain from murder in years to come, and St Keyne well, a draught of whose water ensures that the drinker shall dominate his or her marital partner, providing that the other has not drunk of it first. Other wells of particular interest are St Guron's well, Bodmin; the larger steep-roofed well of St Cleer; the tiny well of St Clether; and the lonely little granite building of St Melor, Cornwall's own child saint. Perhaps most rewarding of all is a visit to St Neot, whose delightful manikin saint subsisted off the fish he caught in his well and whose legends are told in the renowned fifteenth century stained glass windows of the beautiful church of his name.

These numerous men and women whom we call the Cornish saints and around whom so many entrancing legends are woven are of greater significance than the casual visitor may realise; principally to them must be attributed the fact that in Cornwall, unlike the rest of this country, Christianity has an unbroken history of over 1500 years.

Bodmin Moor

The wild expanse of Bodmin Moor is superficially and fleetingly familiar to most visitors to Cornwall, as the main road to the west bisects this area. But by car from a busy road is no way to try and see this unspoiled part of old Cornwall. It is essentially a place for the walker — well-shod, that is — or at least for quieter motoring on its few byways.

The Moor is about a hundred square miles in extent, a miniature Dartmoor lying between Launceston to the east, Bodmin to the west, Camelford to the north and Liskeard approximately to the south. The average elevation is about a thousand feet above sea level rising to a maximum of 1375 ft. This elevation gives a much higher rainfall than places on the coast farther west and also winter temperatures which are equally striking in their difference. Bodmin Moor is in fact more or less the only area in Cornwall where ice and snow occur in many winters. The soil is of a thin and acid nature, with deep peaty quagmires in the hollows between the granite tors, just as on Dartmoor. Cattle are pastured here in summer, together with ponies and sheep, but farms on the true high moor are non-existent.

To some, the bare moorland with its windswept acres of rushes and coarse grass, open and devoid of trees, is not beautiful but it is here that the lonely spirit of the Moor is at its strongest; here, although perhaps only a mile in distance from the crowded A30, one is back in a landscape little changed for many centuries. Bodmin Moor has many close and still undisturbed links with the remote past, for there are numerous tumuli, hut circles and other remnants of primitive man scattered across it. At Trewortha in the east, by the area known as Twelve Men's Moor, is an interesting example of an abandoned medieval hamlet. Hereabouts, too, some alluvial gold was produced.

A view of Phoenix United mine, from Bodmin Moor near Minions

The tors or rocky pinnacles at the summit of the hills all have their distinctive names. In the northern half of the Moor (lying north and west of the A30) the principal ones include Bray Down, Buttern Hill, Brown Willy (1375 ft.) which is the highest point on the Moor and close by it Rough Tor — correctly pronounced to rhyme with cow — which is only a few feet lower. Hawks Tor, close by the old hamlet of Temple, just tops the 1000 ft mark but its appearance is sadly marred by the china clay pit close by. There are other smaller but abandoned pits to the south of here, and also currently worked ones on Stannon Marsh west of Rough Tor, but these are the only encroachments of industry into this otherwise unspoilt upland. Granite has been worked north of Caradon and at De Lank near St Breward but not on a scale to damage the landscape.

On the southern half of the Moor, there are fully as many tors again: Carneglos Tor, Fox Tor, immediately south of the little village of Altarnun, with its church known as the Cathedral of the Moors; the curiously named Browngelly, Newel Tor and Hill Tor, on Smallacoombe Downs; and eastward of them on the opposing slope, Sharp Tor and Kilmar Tor. There is also another Hawks Tor in this half of the Moor, situated near Northill where the beautiful Lynher river flows southward along the edge of the Moor. Caradon Hill more or less marks the southern limit of the moor. Near it is is the celebrated Cheesewring, hard by the now-abandoned granite quarry of the same name; this is perhaps the best known and most photogenic of all the tors on Bodmin Moor.

The various rivers running off the Moor form deep and beautiful wooded valleys which are the perfect foil to the bare moorland above. Apart from the Lynher, already mentioned, there is the river Inny which rises near Davidstowe and runs down almost parallel to the Lynher for some of the way, to join the Tamar. Both are noted for their trout. On the west the valley of the river Camel, winding down from St Breward to near Bodmin, is equally beautiful. But it is on the southern slopes of the Moor that the finest sylvan streams are to be found, by Cardinham and Warleggan and St Neot, where the tributaries of the Fowey come tumbling down to join the main river. Hereabouts is the best woodland scenery in all Cornwall and the Fowey itself can be followed up past Treverbyn and Golytha Falls and so out onto the open moor. A minor road follows its course north to Bolventor where one is back on the A30. The tumbling head waters of the Fowey can be traced on beyond, to their source near Brown Willy. Meanwhile at the lonely hamlet of Bolventor is Jamaica Inn, the old slate-hung haunt of smugglers and highwaymen which is now immortal. To the south, perhaps a mile away, is also Dozmare Pool, Cornwall's largest natural inland lake. Set in a gentle depression 1000 ft above the sea, it is surrounded by a treeless waste of peat and heather. After the rolling expanses of the restless moor, whose wind forever tears the hair and ruffles alike the coarse coats of nibbling sheep and pony, the level lake forms a line of welcome repose, and has an air of tranquil melancholy all its own. There are those who may still believe that the lake is bottomless, for it was this very water that, in Cornish legend, the fearsome and wicked Tregeagle was to ladle out with a holed limpet shell, in eternal penance for his sins. But on more than one occasion, the brimming lake, usually more than filled by the heavy rains of winter, has dried out in an unusually dry summer and the peaty bottom has been laid bare for all to see.

Thereby, perhaps another Cornish legend should have died. For some say that after battle in Cornwall against the heathen English, at the command of the dying King Arthur, his mighty sword Excalibur was flung into this very lake, making 'lightnings in the splendour of the moon'; and thereafter came a dark funeral barge to bear the king away across the water. And, all others being slain, there was left alone upon the shore his one remaining knight, Sir Bedivere, in tears because the Round Table was no more.

The Cheesewring, a strange natural rock formation on the Moor

Gwennap Pit

Carn Marth forms an extension of Carn Brea to the eastward; part of the granite backbone of Cornwall. Near its summit, midway between Redruth and St Day, lies the county's principal place of pilgrimage. This is Gwennap Pit, a massive sunken amphitheatre which is known to Methodists throughout the world.

John Wesley's first visit to the Pit was in September 1762, when this site was chosen for one of his open-air meetings. The shelter it gave from a wild gale then blowing revealed the advantage of this natural amphitheatre and here crowds of miners heard Wesley preach every time he came to Gwennap parish thereafter.

The Pit was, in fact, at that time an irregular 'sink', formed by mine subsidence and by old surface mine workings, being about a hundred yards long and 70 feet or so wide. Wesley was fond of his visits there, speaking of Gwennap Pit as 'far the finest (natural amphitheatre) I know in the kingdom', and in 1806 it was decided to re-model it and create it in the form we know today. The sides of the existing depression were filled in or excavated, as required, to make a circular pit some 120 feet across at the top, sloping down to about 16 feet diameter in the centre. Thirteen steps or terraces were cut, levelled and turfed around it, with a Cornish stone hedge built around the topmost terrace. The newly re-modelled Gwennap Pit was opened at Whitsuntide 1807 and a service has been held there — in peace and in war, in storm or shine — on the anniversary of this event ever since.

John Wesley claimed to have preached to a crowd of no less than 32,000 in the original Pit. This was larger than the one we know today and perhaps this vast concourse did indeed attend. The estimate is now felt to be an exaggeration, however, although it must be remembered that in the early nineteenth century Gwennap was the most populous parish in Cornwall and the miners and their families flocked by the thousand to hear Wesley and others preach there. Many of these people walked from towns and villages miles away to listen.

Well filled, the present Pit holds about 2000, and the annual Whitsun (or Spring Bank Holiday) ceremony there is a part of the Cornish calendar that is deeply and firmly rooted. The Pit has been called, with some justification, the Wesleyan Cathedral of Cornwall, and appropriately enough, in view of its origin as an old tin working, there stands nearby the abandoned Cathedral Mine.

Next page: outside Gwennap Pit, Whit Monday 1910

WHITMONDAY

Cornwall's forgotten ports

The great highway of Cornwall prior to the nineteenth century was provided by the waters around its coasts, while the by-ways lay in the branching inlets of the Fal, the Helford, the Tamar, the Fowey and the Camel rivers. All kinds of merchandise, from seaweed for the fields to massive mine engine parts carried in strengthened ships, travelled by sea wherever possible in this age when land transport by pack animal, stage coach or lumbering waggon was tedious and expensive.

Where no local harbour or quay existed, small sailing vessels would run up onto the beach at high water to be discharged over the side into carts or mule panniers before the next tide. Innumerable coves and open beaches in the West Country regularly saw this practice, with vessels landing coal, limestone, manure and a host of other cargoes. It was, of course a dangerous procedure except in settled weather, many a vessel being lost or damaged as a result of a gale blowing up. In more sheltered waters it was possible to provide small quays to meet very localised demands; it is probable that most waterside farms had one of some sort, whence agricultural produce was taken off to local markets or for trans-shipment, and oreweed, sea-sand, lime and other manures were brought in by barge.

There were, however, many instances in which a proper harbour was required and a number of small ports sprang up to meet these needs, more particularly along those stretches of coast where mines of copper or tin lay close at hand. Some of these ports were destined to disappear almost without trace with the decline in mining. The diminutive harbour of Trevaunance, beneath the cliffs at St Agnes, is a case in point. Here, of necessity, coal and timber were hauled up the cliff in baskets from the schooners berthed beneath, whilst ore was lowered to them in the same way. Built in the eighteenth century to serve the local mines, it was damaged by Atlantic storms again and again but on each occasion was repaired, until such time as its useful life was past. In the 1920s, storm damage to it was left untouched and it was doomed as a result. Today, only a vestige of it remains above the waves, although the outline of the pier and its massive tumbled stones can be discerned in the water below.

Nearby Portreath was a much larger and more important port serving the mines around Redruth. It was once a busy harbour, with two basins which were entirely man-made to create a safe haven. The schooners engaged in the trade with copper ore to Swansea came back with coal for the mine pumping engines. This two-way trade was responsible for many other small ports coming into existence. On the estuary of the Fal, at various now forgotten wharves, a great deal of this trade was carried on, some of it in competition with Portreath. At Restronguet Passage, by the Pandora Inn, there was a copper ore quay; others existed at Point and Devoran; in Pill Creek, at Feock; and at Roundwood, above King Harry Ferry; whilst Newham, immediately below Truro, was a shipping place once much used. Of all these, Devoran was the most important, on account of the railway which ran thence up to the Gwennap-Redruth mines. It is difficult to realise that deep-water schooners and ketches once sailed up to Devoran's now almost vanished wharves, for the estuary is badly silted up. In fact, all the small ports and quays of the Fal have suffered the same fate, the first to succumb being those least scoured by the tides: Perran Wharf; Bissoe, it is said; Tresillian; Ruanlanihorne; Tregoney and even, tradition has it, Grampound, now five miles above the tidal limit.

Apart from Portreath on the north coast, Hayle was once upon a time the busiest of Cornish ports in the coasting trade, whilst Newquay also formerly had considerable commercial maritime activity, chiefly in shipping china-clay. The creeks to the north and south of Newquay — St Columb Porth and the Gannel — were also used for discharging ships, as well as for shipbuilding. Padstow, of course, is still a thriving port, although the present is nothing compared with its heyday, when sailing coasters in the Irish Sea and Bristol Channel trades thronged the quays and when big deep-water barques traded thence to New Brunswick and New York. Padstow also once had pretensions to becoming a major base for the herring fishery, and hopes, too, of becoming a passenger port when the railway came. Farther up the Camel, Wadebridge enjoyed a much greater sea-borne traffic than is now realised, including the shipment of granite from the De Lank quarries and the exporting of many tens of thousands of tons of rich iron ore from mines to the south.

On the south coast of the county, St Michael's Mount — or The Mount, as it was usually called — was a commercial port of some note in former centuries. Copper ore was shipped from there, brought from the mines behind Marazion, and carried over the causeway on pack mules at low water to schooners lying in the shelter of the pier. Timber was landed here, as well as coal and other mine supplies. Porthleven, still a thriving fishing village, was similarly devoted to the mining trade; it also shipped china-clay and china-stone, while from nearby Mullion another raw material for the Staffordshire pottery industry, soapstone from the cliffs close at hand, was exported in the early nineteenth century. In this Lizard area, however, the most interesting port of former days is undoubtedly Gweek. Lying at the tidal limit of the beautiful Helford River, this too was busy with the coming and going of mine supplies and tin from Wendron. Porth

The tiny harbour at Mullion once exported soapstone to Staffordshire

Navas, now the headquarters of the Duchy of Cornwall oyster farms, was also a point of shipment for copper ore up to about 1830.

Farther eastward, south of St Austell and the china-clay country, lies Pentewan, a once busy harbour into which no trading vessel has entered for many a year. To improve an already existing haven, the basin here was excavated in the 1820s and for over a century Pentewan was one of the three ports in St Austell Bay for the shipment of china-clay. Unlike its rivals, however, this port was plagued throughout its existence by silting from waste brought down by the river from the clay pits inland. Charlestown, a short distance to the east, owes even less to nature than Pentewan, being an entirely man-made harbour, built to serve the same industry; it comprises two diminutive basins, the inner one with lock-gates, and is remarkably similar to Amlwch in Anglesey. Small coasters still come into Charlestown, however, and neither it, nor the bustling china-clay port of Par nearby, can be included among the lost ports of Cornwall.

The tinners' parliament

As befitted the principal metalliferous mining district of Britain — indeed, be it said, one of the principal at one time in all Europe — Cornwall had an organised administration, loosely termed the Stannaries, covering all aspects of the tin trade. It had its own laws and customs, its own charter from the Crown and its own small parliament. In this it was unique, although Cornwall has some similarities to other ancient 'free' mining areas, such as the Peak District of Derbyshire and the Forest of Dean.

Tin was an important British industry well before the Norman conquest and the Stannaries were in existence before the end of the twelfth century, at which date Devon was the more important of the two western counties for the metal. The principal official was the Warden, appointed by the King. His chief task was the collection of the tax on tin, as well as controlling the jurisdiction of matters affecting mining. Under him operated a retinue of vice-wardens, court stewards, collectors, controllers and bailiffs.

In 1201 the first charter was issued to the Stannaries, setting out the tinner's rights and his duties in return. Perhaps the two most interesting were that, first the tinners were thereby exempted from the normal laws and taxes which applied to the rest of the community, and secondly, they had the right to search for tin 'without hindrance from any man' on unenclosed land.

The charter of 1201 divided Cornwall into four 'stannaries' or mining districts: Foweymore, corresponding approximately to the present area of Bodmin Moor; Blackmore, the uplands lying to the north of St Austell — once famous for tin and now for china-clay; Tywarnhaile, on the north coast, centred on St Agnes: Penwith and Kerrier, comprising the two united districts of the Land's End and the Wendron area. Each of these stannaries appointed six stannators, and the whole body of these men constituted the Tinners' Parliament, as authorised by their royal charter. Earlier, less organised, parliaments are reputed to have been held in the open air in such places as Caradon Hill and Bodmin Moor, but the true charter parliament met at Lostwithiel in similar fashion to the national one in Westminster, although much less often. The last year in which it sat was 1752.

A law-breaking tinner was brought before the stannary court and, if guilty, served a term of imprisonment in the stannary gaol at Lostwithiel. Further royal charters confirmed and either extended or amended the constitution and administrative powers of the Stannaries. After the fourteenth century, the earldom of Cornwall, held by one or other branch of the royal family, was merged into a duchy and granted to the Prince of Wales. Gradually Cornwall began to approach Devon in the relative importance of its tin output and then to replace it. By the end of the seventeenth century, west Cornwall was also beginning to eclipse the eastern mining districts, and was to become by far the most important well before 1800.

The major part of royal revenue from the Duchy of Cornwall was derived from a duty on the tin produced, the so-called coinage duty. At appointed coinage towns in each of the Stannaries, a corner was struck off the blocks of smelted metal, assayed and then marked with a seal. Then, and then only, could the tin be sold — that is after the coinage duty had also been paid on it. A great deal of tin was clandestinely sold for shipment without paying this duty, a form of 'outward' smuggling which was peculiar to Cornwall.

This coinage process, taking place at regular intervals, was an archaic form of taxing and regulating the Cornish tin trade for the benefit of the heir to the Crown. At coinage time in Truro and Penzance, huge blocks of tin, too heavy to be stolen, littered all the principal streets, with pack animals and carriers' carts coming and going from the coinage hall and the surrounding smelting houses. Ultimately the practice was abolished in 1838, being one of the first reforms in the reign of the young Queen Victoria.

Cornish antiquities

One of the most interesting and singular features of Cornwall is the vast number of its antiquities. There are more readily visible examples of the tombs, monuments and dwellings of early man here than in almost any other county in Britain, and those sensitive to atmosphere will be acutely aware of its haunted quality — at least in the more silent and solitary winter months.

First there are the dolmens and barrows of Stone Age and Bronze Age man, built up to 4000 years ago. The barrows, or burial mounds, are of many types, being made of stones or earth, and in plan oval, round or cigar-shaped. They vary in size from several feet in diameter up to as much as 30 or 40 feet, and occur frequently throughout Cornwall, chiefly on the uplands or the cliffs. Many have disappeared altogether, the earth or stones having been removed during farming operations or for building walls, but good examples of the various types remain.

Ballowal Carn, near St Just, is one of the largest barrows in Cornwall

In some cases, the removal of the covering earth or cairn of stones revealed a stone burial chamber within. These are called quoits or dolmens, and seem to have been associated with cremation rather than inhumation. They consist of one gigantic horizontal slab of stone supported on three or four vertical slabs, this having been raised to that position — usually about six feet off the ground — by manual labour alone. In some cases even those tremendous stones have been removed for other purposes some time in the past. Most tombs of this type lie in West Penwith, the Land's End peninsula; for instance, Lanyon, West Lanyon, Mulfra, Chun, Zennor and Sperris Quoits. All these lie conveniently near together between St Just and Zennor. In east Cornwall is the famous Trethevy Quoit, St Cleer, still standing erect like that at Lanyon. Another most interesting group comprises the so-called chambered tombs of the Isles of Scilly. It is probable that these also all lay under large stone cairns, usually approximately oval or round. Over fifty of these are known, normally occurring in groups of less than four, although a large number lie together on Porth Hellick Down, near St Mary's.

Also of interest and of great antiquity are the seventeen stone circles of Cornwall, which lie chiefly on Bodmin Moor and in Penwith. Their exact purpose is unknown but it is presumed that they performed some religious or ceremonial function. Most have legends attached to them, such as the Nine Maidens — a name given to many of the circles — the Merry Maidens near Lamorna Cove in the Land's End, and the famous Hurlers near the Cheesewring on Bodmin Moor. Close to the Merry Maidens, who were petrified for dancing on the Sabbath, are two menhirs or standing stones, the tallest 15 ft high, called the Pipers. Apparently the two young men who provided the irresistible music met the same fate. There are many menhirs in Cornwall, often standing singly; eighty for example are known in the Land's End peninsula, of which forty are still erect. Their real purpose is not properly known, but a number have been shown to be associated with cremation, as for instance that at Try Farm, near Penzance.

But more is known about the strange, upright holed stones of Cornwall, most famous of which is the Men-an-Tol near Lanyon Quoit. This strange stone is about 4 ft in diameter; through the small hole in the centre little children suffering from scrofula were passed naked, for a certain cure, in none too distant days. Standing between two other upright stones, the Men-an-Tol remains silent about this superstition. Its original function was as an entrance stone to a tomb chamber.

As well as burial mounds and various monuments, the primitive Cornish left many traces of their dwelling houses and forts. Bronze

The Men-an-Tol

Age settlements are common on Bodmin Moor and occasional in Penwith and the Lizard. These people lived in groups of small huts with four-foot high stone walls and roofs probably of thatch; nearby can be seen traces of their tiny walled fields. Nearer to us in time were the Iron Age Celts, light of eyes and hair, who came to Britain across the Channel from the Continent. It is from the Celts and the earlier dark-haired, olive-skinned Mediterranean stock that the Cornish are descended, unlike the English 'foreigners' from up-country. The Celts lived in villages of stone huts with paved floors, of which a very fine example remains at Chysauster, north of Penzance. They built also hill-top fortresses, which were used as places of refuge; these consisted of concentric rings of ditches and walls, remains of which are to be seen at Castle-an-Dinas on the Goss Moor, Carn Brea near Redruth, Chûn Castle near St Just-in-Penwith, and Trencrom Hill south of St Ives. Another type of fortress was the 'cliff castle', always lying on a coastal promontory and simply separated from the mainland by a rampart and ditch or a wall across the neck of land joining the two. Porth Island near Newquay, the Rumps north of the Camel estuary and Cape Cornwall are examples. The Celts constructed also a number of mysterious subterranean chambers with low entrances, very dark and tunnel-like. These were probably places of refuge, used also for storage.

The youngest of Cornish antiquities, erected some time before the fine Cornish crosses of the Middle Ages, are the so-called inscribed stones. Some of these bear a Christian device, and two, still legible after the passage of centuries, are of particular appeal. The Men Scryfa or Stone of Writing, near Morvah in Penwith, is the memorial or gravestone of 'Rialobranus, son of Cunovalus'; and near Hayle another stone tells us that 'Cunaide lies here in the grave. She lived 33 years'. Had there been a date on this headstone, it would have read about A.D. 500.

Cornish crosses

Whereas the Bronze Age peoples erected the menhirs or standing stones which point to the sky everywhere in Cornwall, and the very early Christians set up the various inscribed stones that seem to be a continuation of this custom, so during the Middle Ages hundreds of Cornish crosses were raised up. At least 400 of these remain, not by any means all in churchyards. The secondary purpose of each one cannot be determined but while many clearly mark a holy place and pre-date the church near which they stand, others appear to have been set up in memory of the dead, some as boundary stones, as guide posts at cross roads, and along remote, ancient trackways for wayside devotions. As with earlier antiquities of great interest, most of the crosses lie in the extreme west of the county. Their numbers must at one time have been much greater; the Reformation took its toll, and many more were laboriously shifted over the centuries to serve more practical purposes, crosses having been put to work in walls, hedges, seats, foot-bridges, sundials, bee-hives, as well-covers, pig-troughs, rubbing posts for cattle, and in one case, even as a pivot for a threshing machine.

Most of these crosses are carved out of the intractable grey Cornish granite, and their design and decoration is of infinite variety, although some are very crude and simple. The granite used was that known as moor-stone, that is, natural blocks of the rock lying on the surface, where they could receive their first rough dressing *in situ*. The coarsely crystalline nature of the rock and its hardness did not lend themselves to delicate and intricate carving, and over the centuries their decoration has become even more blunted by the beating of winter rain and gales, remaining nevertheless very satisfying to the eye and to the touch. Most of them are of the Celtic wheel-headed design and there are also examples of four-holed crosses, the granite being pierced right through between the four limbs of the cross.

Interesting examples are found in Mylor churchyard — the largest of all the crosses, with only ten feet of its seventeen foot long shaft above ground; in Padstow churchyard; in Morrab Gardens, Penzance — formerly situated in the town itself and used as a tethering post for pigs; the very fine, beautifully decorated cross in Cardinham churchyard; the four-holed cross at Lanherne, which is of the more easily carved Pentewan stone and is intricately decorated; the very early cross near St Piran's church near Perranporth; and three other crosses not of granite — one of sandstone in Breage churchyard, an elvan cross at Trevena, Tintagel, and one of slate near Tarret Bridge, St Clether.

The dreaded Manacles

Just off Porthoustock, on the southern side of the Helford estuary, lies a group of rocks which are the visible evidence of the terrible Manacles Reef. Each projecting portion of this has its name, all except one being covered at high water. Large vessels always gave the Manacles a wide berth but smaller coasters could, with local knowledge, pass safely in the channel between the reef and the shore. To vessels bound up or down the Channel little hazard was presented unless badly off course coming westward, but in the days of sail very large numbers of vessels entered Falmouth for orders, repairs, trading or on Packet service and having rounded the Lizard to head for the Fal, the Manacles lay as a grave danger to them on their port hand.

The first two serious wrecks known to have taken place here occurred in the winter of 1819, when the naval transports *Dispatch* and *Primrose*, homeward bound from Spain, came to grief. Of the large number who lost their lives on this awful night, 104 are buried in St Keverne churchyard, as is recorded on a memorial tablet within the church. The next major casualty was the emigrant ship *John*,in May 1855, bound to Canada from Plymouth. Out of 286 aboard, only 91 survived this disastrous wreck. Then there was the *Despite* in 1869, the date when a lifeboat was first stationed at Porthoustock, specifically to give coverage to the Manacles area.

In 1898, on 14 October the ss *Mohegan* was approaching the

This is the grave at St Keverne of 106 people who died in the Mohegan, *which struck the Manacles in 1898; the churchyard is full of similar memorials*

Manacles on a voyage from London for New York, with 157 persons aboard including the crew. When on a mistaken course, she steamed onto the reef in the darkness; a gale was blowing and there was a long delay before any of the local lifeboats could locate the wrecked steamer or her boats. As a result, over 100 persons died, adding to the already terrible death roll accountable to this reef.

Only five months later the large three-funnelled liner *Paris* drove onto the rocks on the mainland opposite the Manacles. She carried no less than 756 passengers, and what might have been the worst loss of life of any wreck around the Cornish coast was avoided solely due to the calm weather prevailing at the time the *Paris* struck. Unlike the *Mohegan*, whose remains lie on the submerged reef, she was later salved, to pass the Lizard and the Manacles many times again in her subsequent career.

There had been various suggestions made from time to time to provide navigators with warning of the Manacles reef but nothing more substantial than bell buoys was ever provided. The red sector of St Anthony lighthouse, built in 1835 at the entrance to the Fal, gives additional warning of it, and since the decline in the number of vessels using Falmouth following the disappearance of sail, the reef is no longer the potential hazard it once was.

Pilchard seining

In former centuries, Cornwall's people looked to the sea to provide much of their daily wants. From an early date the autumn shoals of pilchards which visited the county's shores were called upon to provide a great part of the Cornishman's winter diet. Salted down, moreover, the fish — which might be described as a cross between a sardine and a herring — could be stored and used all the year round, whilst extra large catches could be 'pressed' to yield valuable oil, or could be shipped off for export. Seining was the name for this inshore fishing for pilchards and formed for many decades the most important part of Cornwall's fishing industry.

Some pilchards were caught by drift nets, it is true, but seine netting was far and away the principal method in the past. Three boats made up a typical seining 'company': the 'stop' boat, rowed by six men and carrying the massive main net which might be anything from 200 to 400 yards or more in length; the 'follower' boat, of similar size, which carried the tuck net; and lastly the 'lurker' from which the master seiner and others directed the operations — although sometimes this supervision was carried out from the shore. The shoal of pilchards,

33

having been spotted from the nearby cliffs by a 'huer' or watcher, was encircled by the main seine, rowed out and placed round the fish with all possible speed. Capstans on the boats or on shore were then used to haul the net closer together and nearer to the shore. Offshore, the fish were taken from within the seine net by repeated shootings by the smaller 'tuck' seine. With an exceptionally large catch, in calm weather the shoal might be left a few days enclosed by the main seine net moored into position; this enabled the storage and salting down of the pilchards to proceed in the fish cellars on shore. Here the various members who had shares in the seining company divided their catch. Some was sold; some stored in bulk ready for pressing for oil, with the residue sold for manuring the land; the rest was packed in casks between layers of salt either for export or for future consumption.

Quite enormous catches were made on some occasions, resulting in the netting of many millions of fish within a few hours and a considerable export trade grew up in pilchards from Cornwall from the early eighteenth century onwards, to dispose of the surplus over and above that locally consumed. In 1871, for example, 45,683

Tucking pilchards off St Ives, taken about 1900 with an unusual panoramic camera

hogsheads of pilchards were sent abroad, representing the largest quantity at any time in the nineteenth century. Each hogshead contained many thousands of fish. About a century earlier, in the year 1790, the total catch in the county was reported to be 52,000 hogsheads. The great bulk of the pilchard harvest, obtained from July to about the end of the year, was shipped from Penzance or from St Ives to Mediterranean ports, chiefly in Spain or Italy. Later, pilchard cargoes were also sent to the West Indies where there was a similar demand for large quantities of cheap fish — heavily salted to withstand the hot climate — during Lent and on the Roman Catholic Friday.

Seining companies were to be found in every small port and fishing cove all round Cornwall, more particularly on the south coast. In addition to the usual ports one would expect to find prominent — Newlyn, Porthleven, Falmouth, Mevagissey, Fowey, Looe — places such as Gunwalloe, Mullion, Coverack, St Mawes and St Michael's

35

Weighing fish at Polperro about 1870, outside the Three Pilchards Inn

Mount were all centres of seining, whilst eastward it was carried on beyond the borders of Cornwall, at least as far as Bigbury in Devon. On the north coast, Sennen, Portreath, Perranporth, Port Gaverne and Tintagel were similarly active, as well as the principal fishing ports of St Ives, Newquay, Padstow and Port Isaac. Each company had its own distinctive name: the Good Luck Seine at St Mawes, the Venice Seine at Padstow, the Prosperous at Mevagissey, to name but a few.

By the beginning of this century seining in Cornwall was in decline. It had disappeared from many of the smaller coves and, although continued on a lesser scale at all the principal ports, Newlyn had become the main centre of the trade. Drift netting and the rise of more profitable fishing for mackerel and herring, coupled with the somewhat unaccountable disappearance by slow degrees of the pilchard shoals that once had swarmed into west Cornish waters, came to replace seining entirely and by 1930 this once widespread feature of Cornish maritime life had passed into history.

Curious mine names

Scattered throughout Cornwall, more particularly in the parishes west of Truro, are the remains of hundreds of old, abandoned mines. Indeed, these are to be measured in thousands rather than hundreds, worked in the eighteenth and nineteenth century heyday of this historic industry. Lead and copper have been mined extensively as well as tin, including lodes running out to sea beneath the ocean's bed.

The Cornish for mine is 'Wheal' (anciently spelt 'huel'), which literally means 'a working'. Many mines bore personal names, such as Wheal Jane, Wheal Kitty, Wheal Albert and Wheal Henry; others bore the name of the landowner, for instance Wheal Basset or Wheal Vivian. There were also many mines whose names were intended to inspire those concerned with them, of which Wheal Hope and Wheal Confidence are good examples.

But these names, though distinctive, are not so unusual. A list of Cornish mines of former centuries reveals some curiosities which even the mining historian cannot explain: names such as Ting Tang, Ale and Cakes, Blue Hills, Boiling Water, Cook's Kitchen, Ding Dong, Levant and many others. These, it should be stressed, were neither local nor colloquial names but the official names of the mines. Some of them are, while quaintly descriptive, quite understandable, such as Copper Bottom, Tincroft, Hidden Treasure and Copper Hill; others are basically Cornish in origin — Nangiles, Dolcoath, Pednandrea and Polgooth being clearly not of English derivation. From time to time the original source of a mine name is discovered during the course of research but there are literally hundreds which still remain an enigma.

Cornish engine houses

One of the most distinctive man-made features of the landscape of west Cornwall are the ruins of engine-houses that mark the sites of the old mines. These tall, gaunt structures, resembling the ruins of castles, are visible for miles when in an elevated position and are architectural curiosities which have no parallel anywhere else in Britain.

They are the buildings within which were fixed the massive Cornish beam engines used for draining the mine workings. Some of these pumping engines were of great size, with cylinders of 80 inch, 90 inch, and in a few cases even of 100 inch diameter. Working at a slow speed of perhaps six or seven strokes per minute, these engines raised enormous quantities of water from mines 200 or even 300 fathoms

deep and were developed in Victorian times into the most economical mode of mine drainage ever known.

Other similar but smaller beam engines were used for winding ore to surface (known as steam whims) and for stamping it (steam stamps), plus crushers, etc. On a typical nineteenth century tin mine there would be three houses: the largest situated by the shaft, for pumping; one close by for winding; and another in fairly close proximity to operate the stamps. On a big mine there might have been ten or more engines and thus there have been Cornish 'castles' by the thousand. Several hundred still remain today in recognisable form, scattered quite thickly in the mining districts. Many were built of granite, and, being substantial, they have stood the test of time. Most of them, it should be remembered, are more than a century old. The stack, particularly its brick top, is usually the first to go, but the main walls of a big house will probably outlive our children's children.

Two engine houses, complete with their engines, have been preserved at Pool, near Redruth, and can be visited during the summer. One is a winding engine and the other a fine 90 inch, formerly used for pumping.

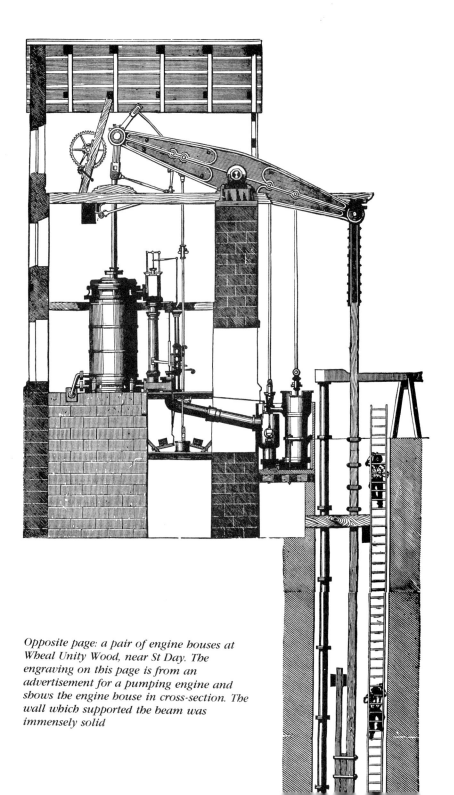

Opposite page: a pair of engine houses at Wheal Unity Wood, near St Day. The engraving on this page is from an advertisement for a pumping engine and shows the engine house in cross-section. The wall which supported the beam was immensely solid

Dolcoath, an engraving published in 1831

Dolcoath — a famous mine

Below the northern slope of Carn Brea, along the length of the former
A30 from Redruth to Camborne, lies one of the principal old mining
districts of Cornwall. Here there were ten or twelve big mines,
including East Pool, Wheal Agar, Carn Brea, South Crofty, Tincroft,
Cook's Kitchen, Dolcoath, North and South Roskear and Wheal Seton,
which lasted through to the end of widespread mining in Cornwall
about 1920.

Most famous of these and celebrated as being the richest of all
Cornish mines, was Dolcoath. Its surface remains, now partly built
over, lie near the railway on the west side of the Red River above
Tuckingmill. At first Dolcoath was primarily a copper mine, worked
from about 1720 onwards, and 160 fathoms deep after half a century.
Working ceased for a few years in the 1790's but was resumed about
1800. It was almost exhausted for copper by the time Queen Victoria
had come to the throne, being then about 270 fathoms deep below
surface. After a decade or so of relative poverty the old mine then
began to show value in tin and by about 1860 the Dolcoath miners had

discovered extremely valuable tin lodes that were to be unequalled anywhere else in Cornwall. Thereafter Dolcoath was, head and shoulders, the principal tin mine in the county, seemingly inexhaustible. In the 1890s a series of underground fires, as well as extensive falls in abandoned workings reaching up into the old copper ground, started a steady decline. Yet until the First World War, Dolcoath continued to be one of the champion mines of Cornwall, and when closed down in the slump of 1920 was 550 fathoms — 3300 feet — deep. This made it by far the deepest mine in the county, and indeed in Britain. During two centuries of almost unbroken working, this small area of ground near Tuckingmill had yielded over £10 million value of ore, and dividends approaching £1½ million — the greatest prize ever in British metal mining.

A great Victorian photographer, JC Burrow, took photographs of the underground workings at Dolcoath and neighbouring mines, and some of these are reproduced in *Cornish Mining — Underground* in the same series as this book.

The dressing floors of Dolcoath in the late nineteenth century, staining the Red River red. Tin mining was never a pretty industry

Padstow's Doom Bar

Along the entire north coast of Cornwall, from St Ives Bay to Welcombe Mouth on the Devon border, there is no safe harbour into which vessels can run during stress of weather. This rocky, inhospitable coast extends for something like eighty miles and in the days of sail represented a hazardous 'leg' in a voyage around the south-west peninsula of England. A map might suggest to a casual observer that the great natural inlet of the Camel estuary would be ideal as a haven for sailing vessels in trouble on this lee shore in westerly gales — particularly as it lies half-way along this otherwise exposed stretch of coast. But this was not the case; indeed the reverse obtained, for the apparent refuge of the Camel estuary was a hidden trap for unsuspecting vessels. Only a narrow deepwater entrance channel existed close under the lee of Stepper Point, the south-western headland; and any captain unaware of this rapidly found his ship drifting or being blown into shallow water on the dreaded Doom Bar.

This bank of sand, exposed at low water, extends across to the Polzeath or eastern shore and it has formed the last resting place of many a sailing vessel. From humble smacks to majestic full riggers, the Doom Bar claimed victims year by year: brigantines and snows, barques and small steamers, sloops and trawlers, plus innumerable coasting schooners. Carew, the seventeenth century historian, summed up Padstow in these words: 'a towne and haven of suteable quality, for both (though bad) are the best that the north Cornish coast possesseth'.

A determined attempt to improve the 'haven' was made in 1829 when a local body was formed, the Padstow Harbour Association for the Preservation of Life and Property from Shipwreck. This installed capstans below Stepper Point, provided a lifeboat, and marker buoys for the channel. A large daymark was also erected on the highest point of the headland. A gratifying number of vessels and their crews were saved by the exertions of this body before it became moribund. Considering the enormous extent of Padstow's maritime trade in the sailing ship era, the wonder is that more vessels were not lost on the Doom Bar.

At high tide on a fine summer's day from either shore we see these innocent waters calm and blue; at low tide, a drying expanse of open golden sand. But this appearance is deceptive, for this is still the Doom Bar of old, the last resting place through the years of literally hundreds of mariners. Local men alone know what conditions can be like in the mouth of the estuary when the westerly gales come round Stepper Point and Trevose: they preserve the memory of the two major

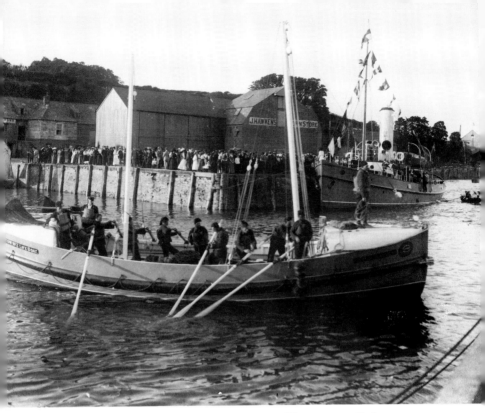

The Padstow lifeboat Edmund Harvey, with its auxiliary tug, on their inaguration in 1901

Padstow lifeboat diasters. In 1865 five were lost when the pulling and sailing lifeboat *Albert Edward* was turned end over end; and in 1900 eight more courageous men when Padstow's big steam lifeboat was capsized.

The Falmouth packets

Falmouth was established as a packet station by the Post Office in 1688, when it was chosen as the English terminus for the recently initiated Spanish mail boat service in the same way that Dover was selected as the station for the Calais Packets, Harwich for those serving northern Europe, and Milford and Holyhead for the Irish mails. Wind and weather permitting — and from Falmouth's splendid land-locked harbour they rarely did not — the packet boats maintained a regular service to Corunna on the north coast of Spain. In 1702, as a result of pressure from the West Indian merchants, packet services were commenced from Falmouth to Jamaica as well as Barbados, while

The packet Westmoreland *beating off a French privateer*

during the eighteenth century similar connections were made with Lisbon, New York, Gibraltar and several ports on the south-east coast of North America — Pensacola, Savannah and Charleston. During the early nineteenth century, packets also ran regularly, usually fortnightly, to Montevideo and Buenos Aires.

The purpose of these vessels was to carry mail and Government despatches, but their commanders, appointed by the Post Office for whom they worked under contract, also received the profit from any passengers carried. At the same time these hired ships carried home diamonds, gold dust and dollars in large quantities, as well as smuggled goods, so that they were frequently intercepted by enemy privateers, or 'Barbary' pirates, and many desperate actions ensued.

By 1827, the establishment was at its peak, 39 vessels with their hired commanders, the senior of whom were always on the Lisbon run, being engaged in this lucrative service. Four years earlier, the control of the whole had passed from the Post Office to the Admiralty, and the hired packets, which were local craft fitted out and manned in Falmouth, were gradually replaced by Admiralty ten-gun brigs, commanded by lieutenants of the Royal Navy. These vessels were fitted out at Devonport, and their stores supplied by a Navy frigate permanently moored in the Carrick Roads with a resulting disastrous loss of trade to Falmouth. These 'coffin' brigs, as they were soon called, were the object of much scorn in Cornwall, since they were badly designed and one after another was lost at sea, together with their crews.

With the advent of steam, the days of Falmouth as a packet port were numbered. Steam packets were less dependent than sail upon the ease of entry to Falmouth harbour in all weathers, and the accessibility of Southampton by rail from London resulted in the transfer of the Ocean Packet Companies to that port in 1843; by 1850 Falmouth had ceased altogether to function as a packet port.

The Great County Adit

Unlike beds of coal or the usually horizontal veins of lead, the lodes (veins) of tin and copper in Cornwall are almost vertical. After only a relatively short period of working, Cornish mines thus become too deep for natural drainage and this problem increases steadily as the lode is followed down. Wherever possible, drainage tunnels, or adits, were driven to unwater mines at as great a depth as possible.

In Cornwall the most important of these was the Great County Adit, which flowed into the upper end of the Carnon Valley near Twelveheads. Unlike most adits this did not serve a single mine but drained thirty or more in the extensive copper mining area between Redruth, Chacewater and Gwennap. From the main line of the adit near its mouth, various branches turned off to north-east and north-west, rather like a tree, with something like 40 miles of tunnels in all. Its average depth is from 120-200 feet (though fathoms are the usual measurement applied) but this increases to over 400 feet at its upper limits. These extend to Pennance mine at the summit of Lanner Hill in the west, to Killifreth Mine near Chacewater to the east, whilst all the mines from Blackwater through Scorrier to Treleigh are also connected on the north. It was thus once possible to descend a shaft close by the east end of Redruth by-pass and work all the way underground almost to Bissoe.

The driving of this adit commenced in 1748 and was continued actively for about a century in its various extensions, and on a lesser scale thereafter until about 1870. At this date most of the Gwennap mines had closed but for some years thereafter the adit was kept in good repair by a committee of mine owners. Ochre and copper precipitated from its mineral impregnated waters were at one time produced in the Carnon valley near Bissoe. The flow from this adit, one of the most extensive mine drainage systems of its kind in Europe, is still considerable, running into the sea at Devoran.

Cornwall's ancient language

The ancient language of Cornwall is a Celtic tongue, originally nearly identical with that formerly spoken in Wales, the Isle of Man and parts of Brittany, and closely linked with the Gaelic of Ireland and the Scottish Highlands. This age-old tongue was almost entirely supplanted in Britain by the successive invasions from the east — Roman, Saxon and Norman — but survived in the western Celtic fringe, although not unsullied. Just as the Celtic tongue in Cornwall had inevitably incorporated some of the language of the earlier people in the county, who came from the Mediterranean, so did it also subsequently absorb some elements of Latin, Anglo-Saxon and French.

The Saxon efforts to subdue the Cornish were prolonged and merciless, and during this time, while the almost legendary King Arthur held out against them, many Cornish took refuge in Brittany or at least in the far west of the county, clinging meanwhile to their Celtic tongue which the Saxons endeavoured to suppress. As a living speech, however, Cornish was doomed; by the choice of English as the official language of Britain in the fourteenth century, by lack of printed books in Cornish, and by the enforcement of the English Prayer Book upon the Cornish after the Reformation, English became the accepted language of the law, the church, the nobility; of commerce and of education. To speak only Cornish was to become a disadvantage and in time to speak only Cornish was a stigma. Only in the Land's End and the Lizard peninsulas, where the Celtic blood remained purest and where past and present were less separated by the events of time, did the ancient tongue survive. Cornish students are now sadly aware of the historical references which mark its gradual disappearance; in 1640 the Sacrament was last administered in Cornish, in St Feock church, south of Truro; by 1650 only the people west of Truro spoke it; in 1678 the last sermon in the language was preached at Landewednack in the Lizard; by 1750 only a handful of people still spoke it in the fastness of Penwith, and Dolly Pentreath, for long erroneously believed to be the last Cornish speaker, died in 1777 at Mousehole.

Since about 1860 there have been attempts to revive the Cornish language, which have gained in intensity in recent decades. These include the resuscitation and publication of various fifteenth and sixteenth century Cornish plays, the compilation of dictionaries and grammars, the introduction of Cornish language classes, church services in Cornish, and the annual Cornish Gorsedd, like those of Brittany and Wales. However much literature may have been written in Cornish, very little has survived; it is known that some of the stories written around King Arthur were Cornish, as was the Tristan and Ysolde legend, so romantically associated with Malpas Passage below Truro; but more substantial are the actual manuscripts of the early Mystery Plays — always performed at the *plen an gwary* or playing place, of which many once existed in the western half of the county. There are also one or two seventeenth century stories, including the famous *Jowan Chy an Horth*, or John of Chyanhor. But that is almost all that remains, apart from traces of the former language both in the vocabulary and syntax of the present Cornish dialect, particularly west of Truro, and elements, too, in many place-names. In addition to the well-known Tre (homestead), Pol (pool) and Pen (headland), other frequent prefixes or suffixes are Wheal (mine working), Chy (house), Ros (moor), Men (stone), Bos (dwelling), Lan (cell or enclosure) and Dynas (fortification).

It is now possible to teach oneself, or be taught, the Cornish language and perhaps re-capture to some extent the idiom and the ancient sing-song speech of Cornwall's remote past and there are a few schools which offer the language as an optional subject. But there are schisms within the revivalist movement, with regard to such major aspects as spelling and grammar, and these schisms threaten the future of the revival.

Even if there can be agreement within the movement, it is probably in the nature of things that Cornish once more would not survive the pressure of 'official' English from up-country, however much this is to be regretted. Cornwall could at best be a bilingual country, and it is common in a bilingual country for the less 'commercial' language to be under constant threat.

Lemmyn, Jowan, ef ny-vynsa servya na fella, mes y fynsa mōs tu ha trē dh'y wrēk. "Nā," yn-meth y vēster, "gwra mōs y'n chȳ, hag yma ow gwrēk-vy ow-pobas myttyn, ha hy a-wra gül tesen ragos, dhe dhōn trē dhe'th whrēk."

Now, John, he would not serve any longer, but would go home to his wife. "Nay," quoth his master, "do thou go into the house, and my wife is baking in the morning and she shall make a cake for thee, to carry home to thy wife."

An extract (with translation) from the seventeenth century Cornish story 'John St Chyanhor'

Other books in this series